From the author of *Enrich Your Life*

Q. T. Archer

The Introvert's Tips to Finding the Perfect Job

GUIDE

Cover Desing and Edited by Mandy L. Parrey

Formatting by Atticus

eBook ISBN 979-8-9912282-5-1

Paperback ISBN 979-8-9912282-4-4

For rights and permissions, please contact:

Aber Stoat Publishing, LLC

2173 Salk Ave, Ste 250

Carlsbad, CA. 92008

hello@aberstoatpublishing.com

http://aberstoatpublishing.com

Contents

Chapter 1

Introduction: Understanding Introversion

and The Importance of Finding the Right Job

I NTROVERSION IS A PERSONALITY trait that manifests itself in various ways depending on the individual. Unlike extroverts, who are energized by social interactions and external stimuli, introverts thrive in more solitary and low-stimulation environments. Understanding introversion is the first step toward navigating the job market effectively for those who identify with this personality trait.

Defining Introversion

The term "introversion" was popularized by Carl Jung in the early 20th century. Introversion is typically characterized by a preference for deeper conversations over small talk, a tendency to think before speaking, and the need for alone time to recharge. It's important to note that introversion is not the same as shyness. While shyness pertains to a fear of social judgment, introverts might enjoy social activities but find them draining after a period of time.

Key Characteristics of Introverts:

1. **Preference for Solitary Activities:** Introverts often enjoy activities that can be done alone or with a close-knit group, such as reading, writing, gardening, or playing musical instruments.

2. **Deep Thought Processes:** Introverts tend to be introspective and reflect on their experiences more profoundly. This enables them to be highly analytical and detail-oriented.

3. **Selective Social Interactions:** They often prefer meaningful one-on-one conversations over large social gatherings. Networking for them involves smaller, well-intentioned circles rather than broad social nets.

4. **Need for Personal Space:** Time alone is critical for introverts to regain their energy. This downtime allows them to process their thoughts and prepare for future interactions.

Psychological and Biological Underpinnings

Recent studies have shown that introversion is rooted both psychologically and biologically. On the neurological level, introverts have different brain pathways than extroverts. Scientists have discovered that introverts exhibit higher cortical arousal, meaning their brains process information more quickly and intensely, leading to a need for less external stimulation.

1. **Neurotransmitter Preferences:** Introverts have a higher sensitivity to the neurotransmitter dopamine, which is linked to reward-seeking behaviors. They find large amounts of external stimulation overwhelming, preferring the neurotransmitter acetylcholine, which is associated with relaxation and a sense of well-being from quiet, reflective activities.

2. **Amygdala Response:** Introverts tend to have a more responsive amygdala, the area of the brain responsible for processing emotional stimuli. This heightened sensitivity makes them more prone to feeling overwhelmed in highly stimulating environments.

3. **Trait Versus State:** Introversion is a trait—a consistent pattern of behavior and thinking. However, the extent to which introversion is expressed can change over the lifetime and can be influenced by situational factors. Therefore, someone might be predominantly introverted but still enjoy occasional extroverted experiences.

Societal Perceptions and Misconceptions

Introversion often faces misconceptions in a predominantly extroverted society that values outgoing and assertive behaviors. Understanding these misconceptions is essential for introverts to leverage their strengths rather than trying to fit into an extroverted mold.

1. **Misconception of Aloofness:** Introverts are often mislabeled as aloof or uninterested. This perception arises because introverts may take longer to engage in conversation fully or may choose not to engage in small talk.

2. **Myth of Incompetency in Leadership:** Society often equates leadership with extroversion. However, numerous studies have shown that introverted leaders are just as effective—if not more so—in certain environments. Leaders like Gandhi, Bill Gates, and Warren Buffett exemplify effective introverted leadership.

3. **Assumption of Weak Communication Skills:** Introverts are sometimes thought to lack communication skills. While they may communicate differently—often preferring written forms or one-to-one conversations—the quality and depth of their communication can be exceptionally high.

Embracing Introversion

For introverts, understanding and embracing their introverted nature can lead to more fulfilling personal and professional lives. This involves recognizing the unique strengths and skills that introversion can bring to work and personal relationships.

1. **Strengths in the Workplace:** Introverts are often excellent listeners, critical thinkers, and observers. These traits can be particularly valuable in careers that require careful consideration and complex problem-solving.

2. **Relationships and Social Interactions:** By focusing on quality over quantity, introverts can build deep, meaningful relationships that are both personally and professionally rewarding.

3. **Self-Acceptance:** Acknowledging and accepting one's introversion can lead to greater self-esteem and well-being. This self-awareness is crucial for finding environments—both personal and professional—that align with their innate preferences.

Practical Tips for Self-Understanding

1. **Personality Assessments:** Tools like the Myers-Briggs Type Indicator (MBTI) or the Big Five Personality Traits can provide insight into one's introversion and other personality facets.

2. **Journaling:** Keeping a journal can help introverts process their thoughts and feelings, leading to a better understanding of their needs and preferences.

3. **Mindfulness Practices:** Activities like meditation and mindfulness can help introverts manage stress and allow for deeper self-reflection.

4. **Physical Health:** Regular exercise and adequate sleep can mitigate the overstimulation that introverts sometimes experience in busy environments.

By understanding what introversion truly means, recognizing the unique qualities and strengths it brings, and embracing one's authentic self, introverts can set a solid foundation on their journey to finding the perfect job. This comprehensive understanding not only enables them to navigate the professional landscape more effectively but also helps them to achieve a balanced and satisfying personal life.

The Importance of Finding the Right Job

Finding the right job is pivotal for anyone, but for introverts, it is particularly crucial. Given their unique preferences and ways of interacting with the world, landing a role that aligns with their personality can significantly impact their job satisfaction, performance, and overall well-being. This section delves into why the right job fit is essential for introverts and how it can influence various aspects of their lives.

Understanding Job Fit

Job fit refers to how well an individual's traits, skills, and interests align with their job's demands and work environment. Good job fit is vital for several reasons, especially for introverts who thrive under certain conditions that may not be present in every workplace.

1. **Productivity and Performance:** When introverts find themselves in roles that match their strengths—like analytical thinking, creativity, or independent work—they are more likely to feel competent and engaged. This alignment leads to higher productivity and better job performance.

2. **Job Satisfaction:** A good job fit contributes significantly to job satisfaction. For introverts, this often means roles that offer quieter work environments, meaningful tasks, and opportunities for independent work. Satisfaction is not merely about avoiding what drains them; it's also about seeking what energizes them.

3. **Work-Life Balance:** Introverts need time outside work to recharge. A job that respects boundaries and promotes a healthy work-life balance ensures that introverts have enough downtime to recuperate, which in turn enhances their productivity and satisfaction.

4. **Career Growth:** When introverts are in roles that suit their skills and preferences, they are more likely to thrive and advance in their careers. The right job acts as a catalyst for professional development and growth.

Impacts of Poor Job Fit

Just as the right job can enhance an introvert's professional life, poor job fit can have a detrimental effect. It's crucial to understand these impacts to appreciate the importance of finding the right job.

1. **Burnout:** Introverts in high-stimulation environments or roles that require constant interaction may experience burnout more quickly than in more suitable roles. Burnout affects not only job performance but also mental and physical health.

2. **Decreased Motivation:** If the job requires skills that the individual does not possess or care about, it leads to a significant drop in motivation. Introverts might find it particularly draining to engage in tasks that do not align with their preferences.

3. **Mental Health Issues:** Poor job fit can contribute to stress, anxiety, and even depression. For introverts, having a job that forces them into uncomfortable social situations frequently can exacerbate these issues, leading to a cycle of stress and dissatisfaction.

4. **Turnover and Job Hopping:** Employees experiencing poor job fit are more likely to leave their positions in search of something better suited to their needs. This can lead to job instability and dissatisfaction.

Characteristics of Ideal Jobs for Introverts

Understanding what makes a job ideal for introverts can guide them in their job search. While every introvert is different, some common characteristics can make a job more favorable.

1. **Opportunities for Independent Work:** Positions that allow for significant individual work time, such as writing, research, or IT development, can be ideal. This independence helps introverts work at their own pace and in their preferred style.

2. **Quiet Work Environments:** Noise and constant activity can be distracting and draining for introverts. Quiet environments, like private offices or jobs that allow remote work, are more conducive to their productivity and well-being.

3. **Deep Focus Tasks:** Jobs requiring deep focus and attention to detail can be particularly fulfilling. Roles in fields like research, data analysis, and technical writing often require this level of concentration.

4. **Limited Social Interaction:** While some level of social interaction is inevitable in most jobs, roles that limit it to essential and meaningful interactions are preferred. Positions that involve one-on-one or small-group collaboration rather than large teams tend to be better suited for introverts.

5. **Meaningful Work:** Work that has a clear impact and aligns with personal values can be fulfilling for introverts. Careers in non-profits, education, and healthcare can often provide this sense of purpose.

Long-Term Benefits of the Right Job Fit

Securing a job that suits their introverted nature offers numerous long-term benefits. These advantages extend beyond mere job satisfaction and permeate various aspects of life, fostering overall well-being.

1. **Enhanced Career Longevity:** When introverts find jobs that suit them well, they're likely to stay longer in those positions, building experience and forging a stable career path. This longevity typically results in better expertise and potentially higher remuneration.

2. **Personal Growth:** Suitable jobs not only cater to an introvert's strengths but also provide opportunities for personal growth. Whether it's taking on new projects that pique their interests or developing new skills at their own pace, the right job nurtures continuous self-development.

3. **Better Work Relationships:** Finding the right job also means being in a work environment that greets an introvert's social preferences more kindly. It encourages healthier, more meaningful work relationships that can enrich their professional and personal lives.

4. **Greater Life Satisfaction:** Finally, job satisfaction heavily influences life satisfaction. When introverts find themselves in roles that suit their personalities, it leads to a positive self-identity, reduced strain between work and life, and an overall happier existence.

Strategies for Finding the Right Job

For introverts embarking on the job search, utilizing specific strategies can make finding the right job more attainable.

1. **Self-Reflection and Assessment:** Before diving into the job market, introverts should take time for self-reflection. Identifying their strengths, preferences, and work styles can pinpoint what types of roles and environments will suit them best.

2. **Research and Networking:** Using online resources to research potential employers and roles can provide insights into what jobs may be suitable. Home in on companies known for their attention to work-life balance, remote work policies, and employee well-being.

3. **Tailored Job Applications:** When applying for jobs, introverts should tailor their resumes and cover letters to emphasize their unique strengths. Highlighting skills such as analytical thinking, problem-solving, and detailed-oriented tasks can make a significant impact.

4. **Interview Preparation:** Preparing for interviews by practicing common questions and considering how to present their introverted traits as strengths can help. Adequate preparation can mitigate anxiety and make them feel more in control.

5. **Leverage Professional Networks:** While networking can be daunting, introverts can use platforms like LinkedIn to connect with industry professionals. Engaging in professional groups and forums can also pave the way for identifying the right job.

In summary, finding the right job is an essential endeavor for introverts, influencing their productivity, satisfaction, and overall well-being. By understanding what constitutes a good job fit, recognizing the potential impacts of poor fit, and utilizing strategic approaches to job searching, introverts can navigate the job market more effectively and secure roles that truly resonate with their nature.

Chapter 2

Identifying Strengths and Weaknesses

and Understanding Your Ideal Work Environment

I N ORDER TO FIND the perfect job, a comprehensive self-assessment is essential. For introverts, understanding their own strengths and weaknesses can provide crucial insights into potential career paths and work environments that will suit them best. Identifying these traits accurately will enable introverts to make informed decisions and highlight their unique capabilities during the job search process.

The Importance of Self-Awareness

Self-awareness is the cornerstone of personal and professional development. For introverts, understanding their natural predispositions can help in selecting roles that not only play to their strengths but also minimize their weaknesses. Self-awareness goes beyond merely knowing one's likes and dislikes; it involves a deep understanding of one's skills, behavioral patterns, and emotional responses.

1. **Enhancing Job Satisfaction:** When individuals have a clear grasp of their strengths, they can seek out roles that allow them to utilize these abilities, leading to greater job satisfaction and engagement.

2. **Improving Performance:** Knowing one's strengths can also inform personal development plans and targeted skill enhancement, leading to improved job performance.

3. **Mitigating Weaknesses:** Awareness of weaknesses enables individuals to seek roles that minimize the impact of these limitations or provides opportunities for skill development to address them.

Methods of Self-Assessment

There are various methods for introverts to assess their strengths and weaknesses. These range from formal assessments to self-reflection exercises, each offering different insights. Utilizing multiple methods can provide a comprehensive view of one's capabilities and potential areas for growth.

1. **Personality and Strengths Assessments:**

- *Myers-Briggs Type Indicator (MBTI):* This widely-used personality assessment helps individuals understand their preferences and behavioral tendencies. For introverts, it can highlight areas such as introverted thinking, sensing, or feeling that influence their work style.

- *StrengthsFinder:* This assessment identifies individual strengths across a range of domains, helping introverts pinpoint their top talents and leverage them in their careers.

- *Big Five Personality Traits:* This model assesses five key dimensions of personality, providing a nuanced view of introversion in relation to other traits like openness, conscientiousness, and agreeableness.

2. **Self-Reflection:**

- *Journaling:* Regular journaling about work experiences can help introverts identify patterns in their behaviors, preferences, and responses to different situations.

- *SWOT Analysis:* Conducting a personal SWOT (Strengths, Weaknesses, Opportunities, Threats) analysis can provide a structured approach to understanding one's abilities and areas for improvement.

- *Feedback from Others:* Seeking feedback from trusted colleagues, mentors, or friends can offer valuable external perspectives on one's strengths and weaknesses.

3. **Professional Guidance:**

- *Career Counseling:* Working with a career counselor can provide expert insights and structured guidance on identifying and leveraging strengths.

- *Mentorship:* Engaging with mentors in one's field can offer personalized advice based on the mentor's experiences and knowledge of the industry.

Common Strengths of Introverts

Introverts possess a range of strengths that can be highly valuable in the workplace. Recognizing and articulating these strengths can enhance confidence and provide direction in the job search process.

1. **Deep Focus and Concentration:** Introverts often excel in tasks that require sustained attention and concentration. Their ability to work diligently and meticulously makes them well-suited for roles in research, writing, programming, and other fields that demand precision.

2. **Analytical Thinking:** Introverts tend to be strong analytical thinkers. They are capable of breaking down complex problems, considering multiple perspectives, and devising well-thought-out solutions. This strength is particularly valuable in fields like data analysis, finance, and strategic planning.

3. **Listening and Empathy:** Introverts are often excellent listeners and can exhibit high levels of empathy. These qualities make them effective in roles that require understanding and addressing the needs of others, such as counseling, human resources, and customer service.

4. **Creativity and Innovation:** Many Introverts are highly creative, enjoying solitary activities that involve imagination and new ideas. Their tendency to think deeply and reflect can lead to unique and innovative solutions in artistic, design, and problem-solving roles.

5. **Independent Work:** Introverts thrive in environments where they can work independently, managing their tasks without constant supervision. Roles that offer autonomy and the ability to manage one's time and projects are particularly appealing.

Common Weaknesses of Introverts

Acknowledging weaknesses is just as important as recognizing strengths. By identifying and understanding their weaknesses, introverts can proactively develop strategies to mitigate their impact on job performance and satisfaction.

1. **Aversion to Networking:** Many introverts dislike traditional networking events, finding them draining and uncomfortable. However, this can be a significant hurdle in career development where networking is crucial.

2. **Discomfort in High-Stimulation Environments:** Introverts often struggle in highly stimulating environments, such as open-plan offices or roles that require constant multitasking and social interaction.

3. **Reluctance to Self-Promote:** Introverts may find self-promotion challenging, feeling uncomfortable highlighting their achievements or speaking up in meetings. This can impact their visibility and recognition in the workplace.

4. **Overthinking Decisions:** Introverts may tend to overanalyze and second-guess their decisions, leading to delays and potential missed opportunities. This can be problematic in fast-paced work environments that require quick decision-making.

5. **Limited Social Engagement:** While deep and meaningful relationships are a strength, introverts may find it difficult to engage in broader social interactions or team activities, potentially affecting collaboration and team dynamics.

Developing Strategies to Leverage Strengths and Mitigate Weaknesses

Armed with a clear understanding of their strengths and weaknesses, introverts can develop strategies to leverage their abilities and address their limitations effectively.

1. **Leveraging Strengths:**

- *Focus on Strength-Based Roles:* Seek out roles that naturally align with one's strengths, ensuring that the job demands match the individual's capabilities.

- *Highlight Strengths in Applications:* Clearly articulate strengths in resumes and cover letters, providing concrete examples of how these abilities have been applied successfully in previous roles.

- *Pursue Skill Enhancement:* Continuously develop strengths through professional development opportunities, training, and skill-enhancement programs.

2. **Mitigating Weaknesses:**

- *Develop Networking Skills:* Gradually expose oneself to networking opportunities, starting with smaller, less intimidating settings. Utilize online platforms to connect with professionals and build meaningful networks.

- *Create Comfortable Workspaces:* Where possible, arrange the work environment to minimize overstimulation, such as using noise-cancelling headphones, requesting flexible work hours, or working remotely.

- *Learn Self-Promotion Techniques:* Practice the art of self-promotion in a manner that feels authentic. This might involve preparing concise summaries of achievements or seeking out mentors who can advocate on one's behalf.

- *Streamline Decision-Making:* Develop decision-making frameworks to avoid overthinking. Setting clear criteria and timelines can help streamline the process.

- *Enhance Social Skills:* Engage in social settings that feel natural, gradually increasing the scope of social interactions. Practice active participation in team activities and seek collaborative projects that align with personal interests.

Case Studies

Real-world examples can provide valuable insights into how introverts have successfully navigated their career paths by leveraging their strengths and addressing their weaknesses.

Case Study 1: Sarah, the Analytical Thinker

Sarah, an introvert with a strong analytical mindset, found her niche as a data analyst. Initially, she struggled with the networking demands of her role but gradually built a network through online forums and professional groups. By focusing on her strengths in data interpretation and problem-solving, Sarah became a valuable asset to her team, and her contributions were recognized through quarterly performance reviews. Sarah also worked on her self-promotion skills, preparing concise presentations that highlighted her achievements and contributions.

Case Study 2: John, the Independent Creator

John, a creative introvert, excelled in solitary work and found his passion as a freelance graphic designer. He initially faced challenges with self-promotion but developed a portfolio website that showcased his work. By leveraging online platforms to connect with clients, John built a thriving freelance business. He organized his work environment to minimize distractions, creating a space that fostered creativity and deep focus. John also set clear boundaries on client interactions, ensuring he maintained a healthy work-life balance.

By identifying strengths and weaknesses, Sarah and John were able to tailor their career paths to their unique abilities and preferences, achieving professional success and personal fulfillment.

In conclusion, self-assessment is a vital process for introverts seeking to find the perfect job. Identifying strengths and weaknesses provides the foundation for making informed career decisions, optimizing job satisfaction, and enhancing overall performance. By leveraging their strengths and developing strategies to address their weaknesses, introverts can navigate the job market more effectively and find roles that truly align with their nature.

Understanding Your Ideal Work Environment

For introverts, finding the ideal work environment is paramount. This extends beyond the scope of specific job roles to the broader context in which they are performed. The ideal work environment can significantly influence an introvert's productivity, job satisfaction, and overall well-being. This section provides comprehensive insights into what constitutes an ideal work environment for introverts and how it can be identified.

The Importance of Work Environment for Introverts

The work environment encompasses the physical, social, and organizational settings in which tasks are performed. For introverts, certain types of environments can either enhance their productivity and job satisfaction or contribute to stress and burnout.

1. **Productivity and Focus:** A suitable environment can enhance an introvert's ability to concentrate on tasks, resulting in higher productivity and better quality work.

2. **Job Satisfaction:** When the work environment aligns with an introvert's preferences, it can lead to higher job satisfaction. The right setting can make work more enjoyable and fulfilling.

3. **Mental and Emotional Well-being:** A favorable environment minimizes stress and overstimulation, contributing to better mental and emotional health for introverts.

4. **Work-Life Balance:** An environment that respects boundaries and provides flexibility can help introverts maintain a healthy work-life balance, ensuring they have enough downtime to recharge.

Physical Work Environment

The physical aspects of the work environment play a crucial role in an introvert's comfort and productivity. This includes the layout, noise levels, and available resources.

1. **Office Layout:**

   - *Private Spaces:* Introverts often thrive in environments where they have access to private or semi-private workspaces. Cubicles, private offices, or designated quiet areas can provide the solitude necessary for deep focus.

- *Remote Work:* The option to work remotely, either full-time or part-time, can be highly beneficial. Remote work allows introverts to create a personalized and quiet workspace at home, free from the typical distractions of an office.

- *Co-Working Spaces:* For those who require occasional interaction but prefer a quiet setting, co-working spaces with designated quiet areas can be ideal. These spaces offer a blend of social interaction and solitude.

2. Noise Levels:

- *Noise Reduction:* Excessive noise can be particularly distracting and stressful for introverts. Work environments that offer noise-reducing solutions, such as soundproof rooms, noise-canceling headphones, or quiet zones, can significantly enhance productivity.

- *Ambient Sounds:* Some introverts may find low-level ambient sounds soothing. Background music or white noise can sometimes help maintain concentration without being overstimulating.

3. Ergonomic and Health Factors:

- *Comfortable Furniture:* Ergonomic chairs, desks at appropriate heights, and comfortable seating arrangements can support better posture and physical health, reducing discomfort and enhancing focus.

- *Lighting and Ventilation:* Natural light and good air quality can improve mood and energy levels. Environments with adjustable lighting and proper ventilation are ideal for creating a comfortable workspace.

Social Work Environment

The social dynamics within a workplace are equally important for introverts. The way interactions are structured and the culture of the organization can significantly influence an introvert's job satisfaction.

1. Interaction Styles:

- *Purposeful Meetings:* Introverts typically prefer meetings that are structured and goal-oriented. Clear agendas and concise discussions make the best use of time and reduce unnecessary socializing.

- *Small Group Interactions:* Introverts often thrive in settings that favor small group interactions or one-on-one meetings over large gatherings. These interactions are more meaningful and less overwhelming.

- *Written Communication:* Many introverts feel more comfortable with written communication. Email, messaging apps, and project management tools provide a way to communicate effectively without the pressure of face-to-face or phone conversations.

2. Organizational Culture:

- *Inclusivity:* An inclusive culture that values diverse communication styles and personalities can make introverts feel more comfortable and valued. Encouraging participation in a way that respects individual preferences fosters a supportive environment.

- *Respect for Boundaries:* Organizations that respect personal boundaries and offer a degree of flexibility in social engagements and work hours create a more comfortable atmosphere for introverts.

- *Autonomy and Trust:* Trusting employees to manage their own time and projects without constant supervision aligns well with introverted preferences for independent work.

Organizational Work Environment

The structural and policy-related aspects of an organization also play a significant role in creating an ideal work environment for introverts.

1. Flexible Work Arrangements:

- *Telecommuting Options:* Providing options for telecommuting allows introverts to work in environments where they feel most comfortable, which can boost productivity and job satisfaction.

- *Flexible Scheduling:* Allowing flexible work hours enables introverts to work during times when they are most productive, which can vary for each individual.

2. Career Development Opportunities:

- *Skill-Based Training:* Offering training programs that cater to individual strengths and interests supports professional growth. Introverts may prefer online or self-paced training modules that allow them to learn independently.

- *Mentorship Programs:* Access to mentors who understand and appreciate the introvert's approach can provide valuable guidance and support. These programs facilitate professional growth and confidence.

3. Feedback and Recognition:

- *Constructive Feedback:* Introverts tend to appreciate feedback that is constructive and delivered in a private setting. This approach allows them to reflect and make improvements without the anxiety of public criticism.

- *Recognition Programs:* Recognizing achievements in a way that respects the individual's preferences is important. Personal notes, private acknowledgments, or highlighting contributions during team meetings can be more meaningful to introverts than public accolades.

Identifying Your Ideal Work Environment

Understanding what constitutes an ideal work environment for you as an introvert involves a combination of self-assessment and research. Here are some steps to identify and secure the right environment:

1. Self-Assessment:

- *Reflect on Past Experiences:* Consider previous work environments and identify what aspects you found most and least favorable. This will help pinpoint specific needs and preferences.

- *Prioritize Needs:* Make a list of must-haves and nice-to-haves in a work environment. This could include factors like the amount of social interaction, noise levels, and availability of private workspaces.

2. Research Potential Employers:

- *Employer Reviews:* Websites like Glassdoor and Indeed provide employee reviews that can offer insights into the company culture, work environment, and management practices.

- *Company Policies:* Look for information on the company's policies regarding remote work, flexible hours, and workspace arrangements. Many companies list these details on their websites or during the application process.

3. Networking and Informational Interviews:

- *Connect with Employees:* Reach out to current or former employees to gather firsthand information about the work environment. Informational interviews can be an excellent way to learn about the day-to-day atmosphere and management styles.

- *Professional Networks:* Use professional networks like LinkedIn to connect with industry individuals and gather insights. Forums and industry-specific groups can also provide valuable information.

4. Ask During Interviews:

- *Inquire About Work Environment:* During job interviews, ask specific questions about the work environment. Inquire about the office layout, team interaction styles, and policies on remote work and flexibility.

- *Assess Cultural Fit:* Use the interview process to gauge whether the company culture aligns with your preferences. Consider how the interviewers describe their work environment and their responses to your questions.

5. Trial Periods and Contract Work:

- *Consider Short-Term Contracts:* If possible, consider starting with a short-term contract or probationary period. This allows you to experience the work environment firsthand before committing long-term.

- *Freelance and Consulting:* Freelance or consulting roles can offer flexibility and the opportunity to work in various environments, helping you identify what works best for you.

Adapting to the Work Environment

Once you've identified and secured a role, it's important to actively adapt and optimize the work environment to suit your needs.

1. Customize Your Workspace:

- *Personalize:* Personalize your workspace with items that make you feel comfortable and focused. This might include ergonomic accessories, plants, or personal mementos.

- *Organize:* Maintain an organized workspace to minimize distractions. A clean and clutter-free environment can enhance focus and productivity.

2. Set Boundaries:

- *Manage Interruptions:* Politely communicate your need for focused work time to colleagues. Use signals like "do not disturb" signs or designated quiet hours to minimize interruptions.

- *Schedule Breaks:* Take regular breaks to recharge, especially if you are in a high-stimulation environment. Step outside, go for a walk, or find a quiet space to relax.

3. Leverage Technology:

- *Use Productivity Tools:* Utilize tools and apps that help manage tasks and communication. Project management software, calendar apps, and task lists can help keep you organized.

- *Explore Communication Options:* Use various communication tools to find what works best for you. Instant messaging, video calls, or email can be adjusted to suit your comfort level.

4. Seek Support:

- *Communicate with Management:* Keep open lines of communication with your manager about your work preferences and any adjustments that can be made to improve your environment.

- *Engage in Employee Resource Groups:* Many organizations have employee resource groups (ERGs) that provide support and networking opportunities. Joining an ERG focused on introverts or diversity can offer additional support.

Real-World Examples

Real-world examples illustrate how introverts have successfully found and adapted to their ideal work environments, offering practical insights and inspiration.

Example 1: Emily, the Remote Researcher

Emily, an introvert, found her ideal work environment as a remote market researcher. The flexibility of remote work allowed her to create a quiet and personalized workspace at home. She scheduled regular breaks to manage her energy levels and used project management tools to stay organized. Communication was primarily through email and instant messaging, reducing the need for frequent face-to-face interactions. Emily's productivity and job satisfaction soared in this environment.

Example 2: Michael, the Private Office Advocate

Michael, an introvert working as a software developer, advocated for a private office at his company. He explained how a quiet, private space would enhance his focus and productivity to his manager. The company accommodated his request, providing a small office space where Michael could work without interruptions. He customized his office with ergonomic furniture and organized his tasks efficiently. This change significantly improved Michael's performance and job satisfaction.

Conclusion

Understanding and identifying the ideal work environment is a critical step for introverts in finding the perfect job. By considering the physical, social, and organizational aspects of the work environment, introverts can identify settings that enhance their productivity, job satisfaction, and overall well-being. Utilizing self-assessment, research, and proactive adaptation strategies, introverts can secure and thrive in environments that align with their unique preferences and strengths.

Chapter 3

Types of Jobs Suited for Introverts

and Utilizing Online Resources and Networks

F OR INDIVIDUALS WHO IDENTIFY as introverts, finding a job that aligns with their personality can significantly improve job satisfaction and overall well-being. Introverts often thrive in careers that provide ample opportunities for solitary work, deep focus, and meaningful, less frequent interactions. The following sections explore various types of jobs that are particularly well-suited for introverts, categorized based on the nature of the work and the specific needs of introverted individuals.

Creative Professions

Creative professions offer introverts the chance to work independently while utilizing their often exceptional ability to concentrate deeply and think outside the box. These jobs typically allow for quiet and reflective working conditions, which are ideal for introverts.

- **Writer/Author:** Writing is a solitary activity that requires deep thought, creativity, and attention to detail. Whether crafting novels, articles, blogs, or technical documents, writers can work independently and often from the comfort of their own home. Many writers find fulfillment in their ability to express complex ideas and narratives through text.

- **Graphic Designer:** Graphic design involves creating visual content to communicate messages. This role often provides the ability to work independently on creative projects, whether at home or in a quiet office setting. Collaborative aspects of the job are usually limited to discussions with clients or team members, which can often be conducted via email or in small meetings.

- **Photographer:** Photography combines artistic vision with technical skill. While photographers may need to interact with clients occasionally, much of their time is spent behind the camera or editing images alone. The solitude and focus required to capture and refine images align well with introverted preferences.

Analytical and Technical Roles

Analytical and technical roles cater to introverts' strengths in deep focus, attention to detail, and problem-solving. These jobs often involve working independently on complex problems and contribute significantly to an organization's success.

- **Data Analyst:** Data analysts examine and interpret complex data to help organizations make informed business decisions. This role involves substantial amounts of independent work focused on analyzing data sets, building models, and generating reports. Interaction with others is usually limited to presenting findings or collaborating with team members on specific projects.

- **Software Developer/Programmer:** Given their aptitude for focused and detailed work, introverts often excel in software development. This job involves writing and testing code, developing software applications, and solving technical problems. While collaboration does occur, particularly in agile development teams, it generally consists of structured and meaningful interactions.

- **Research Scientist:** Research scientists conduct experiments and analyze results to advance knowledge in their field. The work often takes place in a laboratory or office setting, where scientists can concentrate on their tasks. Collaboration is typically limited to small research teams, peer reviews, and presentations of findings.

Healthcare and Counseling

Healthcare and counseling roles can be highly rewarding for introverts who are empathetic and enjoy one-on-one interactions. These positions often allow for deep, meaningful connections with individuals rather than broad, superficial interactions.

- **Clinical Psychologist/Counselor:** These roles involve working closely with individuals or small groups to provide mental health support and guidance.

Clinical psychologists and counselors conduct assessments, offer therapy, and develop treatment plans, working in quiet, controlled environments that promote privacy and reflection.

- **Medical Laboratory Technician:** Technicians and technologists work behind the scenes to analyze biological samples and support the diagnostic process. This role involves meticulous, solitary work in a laboratory setting, with limited interaction with patients or other staff members.

- **Occupational Therapist:** Occupational therapists help patients develop, recover, and improve the skills needed for daily living and working. This role offers the opportunity to build close relationships with clients through personalized therapy sessions, which is ideal for introverts who value deep, meaningful connections.

Business and Administrative Roles

Introverts can thrive in business and administrative roles that require thorough planning, organization, and attention to detail. These jobs often provide a balance of independent work and controlled, purposeful interactions.

- **Accountant:** Accountants manage financial records, prepare reports, and ensure compliance with laws and regulations. This role demands precision and attention to detail, with much of the work being performed independently. Client meetings and team interactions are typically structured and focused on specific financial tasks.

- **Technical Writer:** Technical writers create user manuals, guides, and documentation for various products and services. This role involves translating complex information into clear, concise text and often requires deep focus and independent work. Interaction with engineers or subject matter experts is usually limited to gathering necessary information.

- **Administrative Assistant:** Administrative assistants support the efficient operation of an office by handling various tasks such as scheduling, correspondence, and record-keeping. Introverts in this role often find satisfaction in organizing and managing information, with interactions limited to necessary communications to keep operations running smoothly.

Remote and Freelance Opportunities

With the rise of digital technology, many introverts are finding success in remote or freelance work. These opportunities allow them to control their work environment and schedule, minimizing unnecessary interactions and distractions.

- **Freelance Writer:** Freelance writers cover a broad array of topics and formats, from content marketing to academic research. This role offers immense flexibility in choosing when and where to work. Freelance writers communicate primarily through email or messaging platforms, allowing for focused, interruption-free work time.

- **Virtual Assistant:** Virtual assistants provide administrative support to businesses or entrepreneurs from a remote location. Tasks can include managing emails, scheduling appointments, and conducting research. This role allows introverts to work independently while offering the flexibility to set their hours and choose their clients.

- **Online Tutor/Instructor:** Teaching and tutoring in a virtual setting enable introverts to share their expertise without the need for face-to-face interaction. Online platforms provide tools for conducting one-on-one or small group lessons, allowing for deep, focused interactions without the stress of managing large classrooms.

Artistic and Fine Arts

Artistic and fine arts careers offer introverts the chance to express themselves creatively while often working independently. These roles are ideal for individuals who find joy in solitary creative processes or prefer communicating through their art.

- **Painter/Illustrator:** Artists like painters and illustrators spend a significant amount of their time working alone on their craft. Whether creating commissioned works or pursuing personal projects, these roles necessitate solitude and concentration, aligning well with introverted preferences.

- **Sculptor:** Sculptors work with various materials to create three-dimensional art.

This role involves extensive planning, designing, and crafting, often in a private studio setting. Interaction with clients or gallery representatives is usually limited and focused on specific works.

- **Craftsperson:** Craftspeople create handmade items such as jewelry, pottery, or furniture. This work requires skill, creativity, and patience, often performed in a quiet, personal workspace. Marketplaces, online stores, and local shows provide avenues for selling creations without requiring constant social interaction.

Science and Engineering

Science and engineering roles can be particularly well-suited for introverts who enjoy problem-solving, innovation, and detailed work. These professions often involve significant independent work and collaboration with small, specialized teams.

- **Environmental Scientist:** Environmental scientists study and develop solutions to environmental problems. Much of their work involves field research, data analysis, and report writing, often performed independently or in small teams. This role allows introverts to contribute to important environmental causes while working in environments that suit their preferences.

- **Civil Engineer:** Civil engineers design, construct, and maintain infrastructure projects such as roads, bridges, and buildings. This role requires a strong analytical mind and attention to detail. While civil engineers do collaborate with other engineers and stakeholders, much of the work involves focused planning and technical design.

- **Biochemist:** Biochemists study the chemical processes within living organisms, conducting experiments and analyzing data to contribute to scientific understanding and medical advancements. This role involves extensive lab work, allowing introverts to focus deeply on their research.

Information Technology

Information technology (IT) careers are well-suited for introverts due to the focus on technical skills, problem-solving, and often substantial amounts of independent work. The IT field is broad and offers numerous paths for introverts to thrive.

- **System Administrator:** System administrators manage and maintain an organization's IT infrastructure. This role involves monitoring system performance, troubleshooting issues, and ensuring network security. Working primarily independently, system administrators may communicate with other IT staff as needed but spend most of their time focused on technical tasks.

- **Database Administrator:** Database administrators ensure that an organization's data is stored, organized, and managed effectively. They perform tasks such as database maintenance, backup, security, and performance tuning. This role requires meticulous attention to detail and can be performed in a quiet, focused environment.

- **Cybersecurity Analyst:** Cybersecurity analysts protect an organization's systems and data from cyber threats. This role involves monitoring networks, analyzing threats, and implementing security measures. Much of the work is performed independently, with occasional team collaboration on larger security initiatives.

Education and Training

Introverts who are passionate about educating others can find fulfilling roles in education and training, particularly in settings that allow for focused and dedicated teaching relationships.

- **Librarian:** Librarians manage library resources, assist patrons, and organize information systems. This role provides a quiet and orderly work environment, ideal for introverts, and involves helping individuals find information, coordinating educational programs, and managing collections.

- **Academic Researcher:** Academic researchers conduct studies and investigations within universities or research institutions. This role involves extensive reading, writing, and data analysis, often performed independently. Researchers also have the opportunity to collaborate with colleagues on specialized projects.

- **Special Education Teacher:** Special education teachers work with students who have various learning disabilities or special needs. This role allows for one-on-one or small group instruction, providing focused and meaningful interactions with students. The work often involves developing personalized teaching plans and materials tailored to individual needs.

Conclusion

Recognizing the types of jobs that are well-suited for introverts is essential for career satisfaction and success. By choosing roles that align with their natural tendencies and strengths, introverts can thrive in environments that support their need for independent work, deep focus, and meaningful interactions. Each of these career paths offers unique opportunities for introverts to leverage their skills and contribute effectively while maintaining their well-being. Whether in creative fields, technical roles, healthcare, or education, the right job can provide a fulfilling and rewarding professional journey for introverts.

Utilizing Online Resources and Networks

In the modern job market, leveraging online resources and networks has become indispensable, particularly for introverts who may prefer less direct forms of networking and research. The digital age offers a wealth of tools and platforms that can help introverts find the perfect job without the overwhelming need for in-person interactions. This section provides a comprehensive guide on how to effectively utilize online resources and networks to optimize the job search process.

Identifying Relevant Job Search Websites

Introverts can benefit greatly from using job search websites tailored to finding roles that match their specific strengths and preferences. Here are several types of job search websites to consider:

1. **General Job Boards:**

    - *LinkedIn:* As one of the largest professional networking sites, LinkedIn provides extensive job listings, networking opportunities, and industry insights. Users can tailor their profiles to emphasize their skills and find jobs that match their qualifications.

    - *Indeed:* Indeed aggregates job listings from various sources, offering a wide range of opportunities. The site allows users to set up job alerts and apply directly through the platform.

    - *Glassdoor:* Besides job listings, Glassdoor provides company reviews, salary information, and interview tips, helping introverts gain insights into potential employers and work environments.

2. **Niche Job Boards:**

    - *FlexJobs:* This site specializes in remote and flexible job opportunities, which can be ideal for introverts seeking roles that allow for solitary and focused work from home.

    - *We Work Remotely:* Another excellent resource for finding remote job opportunities across various industries, We Work Remotely caters explicitly to those looking for roles outside the traditional office environment.

- *AngelList:* For introverts interested in startups, AngelList offers job listings and information about startup companies, including remote positions and flexible work arrangements.

3. Industry-Specific Job Boards:

- *MediaBistro:* Tailored for professionals in media, marketing, and publishing, MediaBistro offers job listings and career resources that can benefit introverts looking for creative and analytical roles.

- *Dice:* Targeting technology professionals, Dice lists job opportunities in IT, software development, and other tech-related fields, where deep focus and technical skills are highly valued.

- *HigherEdJobs:* Catering to academic professionals, this site offers job listings for faculty, administrative, and research positions in higher education institutions.

Utilizing Professional Networking Sites

Professional networking sites are powerful tools for introverts to build connections, seek advice, and uncover job opportunities without the need for extensive in-person networking.

1. LinkedIn:

- *Profile Optimization:* Introverts should craft detailed and compelling LinkedIn profiles, highlighting skills, experiences, and accomplishments. Including a professional photo, detailed work history, and endorsements can enhance visibility.

- *Networking Strategies:* Introverts can connect with colleagues, alumni, and industry professionals by sending personalized connection requests. Joining relevant LinkedIn groups and participating in discussions can also help build a professional network organically.

- *Job Search Features:* LinkedIn's job search tool allows users to apply directly to job listings, set up custom job alerts, and view mutual connections within organizations to facilitate introductions.

2. **Alumni Networks:**

- Many universities and colleges offer online alumni networks that provide job boards, mentorship opportunities, and professional development resources. Introverts can leverage these networks to connect with fellow alumni working in their desired fields, gaining insights and job referrals.

3. **Industry Forums and Groups:**

- *Reddit:* Subreddits like r/careeradvice, r/jobs, and industry-specific communities offer advice, job leads, and discussions about trends and opportunities in various fields.

- *Professional Associations:* Many professional associations have online forums and job boards exclusive to members. Joining these associations can provide access to specialized networks and resources.

Engaging with Online Job Fairs and Webinars

Online job fairs and webinars provide opportunities for introverts to connect with employers, learn about industry trends, and develop skills from the comfort of their own spaces.

1. **Virtual Job Fairs:**

- *How to Participate:* Register for virtual job fairs that align with your career interests. Prepare by researching participating companies, updating your resume, and having a professional profile ready on platforms hosting the event.

- *Navigating the Event:* Use chat features and virtual booths to engage with recruiters and learn about job opportunities. Many virtual job fairs also offer webinars and panel discussions, which can provide valuable insights.

- *Follow-Up:* After the event, follow up with contacts made during the fair through email or LinkedIn to express interest and solidify connections.

2. **Webinars and Online Workshops:**

- *Finding Relevant Webinars:* Search for webinars related to your field of interest through professional associations, LinkedIn events, and educational platforms like Coursera or Udemy.

- *Active Participation:* Engage by asking questions in chat boxes, participating in Q&A sessions, and connecting with speakers and fellow attendees through LinkedIn.

- *Continuous Learning:* Attend workshops and webinars focused on skill development, industry trends, and job search strategies to stay competitive and knowledgeable about your field.

Using Online Career Assessment Tools

Online career assessment tools can help introverts identify their strengths, preferences, and suitable career paths, providing a personalized approach to job searching.

1. Assessment Platforms:

- *Myers-Briggs Type Indicator (MBTI):* This personality assessment helps identify your introverted traits and how they align with various career options.

- *StrengthsFinder:* This tool highlights your top strengths, enabling you to focus on roles that utilize your natural abilities.

- *CareerExplorer:* Offering a comprehensive career assessment, CareerExplorer suggests job roles based on personality, skills, and interests.

2. Interpreting Results:

- Understand how your unique traits can be leveraged in different job roles. Use the results to narrow down job opportunities that align with your strengths and preferences.

Building an Online Portfolio

For introverts in creative and technical fields, an online portfolio can showcase skills and accomplishments, serving as a powerful tool in the job application process.

1. **Creating the Portfolio:**

- *Platform Selection:* Choose a platform such as personal websites (WordPress, Squarespace), portfolio sites (Behance, Dribbble), or GitHub for technical projects.

- *Content:* Include samples of your best work, detailed project descriptions, case studies, testimonials, and a professional bio. Make sure the portfolio is well-organized and visually appealing.

2. **Promoting the Portfolio:**

- *Networking and Applications:* Share your portfolio link in job applications, LinkedIn profiles, and during networking opportunities to provide a comprehensive view of your capabilities.

- *SEO Optimization:* Use keywords related to your skills and industry to improve the visibility of your portfolio in search results.

Utilizing Freelance and Gig Platforms

Freelance and gig platforms offer introverts the flexibility to find work that suits their schedules and working preferences while building a portfolio of experience.

1. **Popular Platforms:**

- *Upwork:* Connects freelancers with clients looking for a range of services, from writing and design to programming and marketing.

- *Fiverr:* Allows freelancers to offer specific services (gigs) starting at $5. Freelancers can build profiles that include reviews, service packages, and past work samples.

- *Freelancer.com:* Offers job listings across various fields, allowing freelancers to bid on projects.

2. **Creating a Strong Profile:**

- Highlight your skills, experience, and a portfolio of past work. Ensure your profile is professional and aligns with the types of gigs you're seeking.

- Collect client reviews and feedback to build credibility on the platform.

Navigating Social Media for Job Searching

Social media platforms like Twitter, Facebook, and specialized forums can be valuable for finding job leads, networking, and staying informed about industry trends.

1. **X aka Twitter:**

- *Follow Industry Leaders:* Follow companies, industry leaders, and job search accounts. Participate in Twitter chats and use hashtags like #JobSearch, #Hiring, and industry-specific tags.

- *Engage and Share:* Share relevant content, engage with posts, and retweet job opportunities. This can increase your visibility to potential employers and industry professionals.

2. **Facebook:**

- *Join Groups:* Join industry-specific Facebook groups where job postings and networking opportunities are shared.

- *Follow Companies:* Like and follow pages of companies you're interested in to stay updated on job openings and company news.

Leveraging Online Learning Platforms for Skill Development

Continuous learning and skill development are crucial in staying competitive in the job market. Online learning platforms provide accessible and flexible options for gaining new skills and qualifications.

1. **Popular Platforms:**

- *Coursera:* Offers courses from top universities and institutions across various fields, with options for free and paid courses leading to certifications.

- *Udemy:* Provides a wide range of courses, often at affordable prices, on technical skills, creative arts, business, and more.

- *edX:* Similar to Coursera, edX offers courses and programs from universities that can lead to certificates or even degrees.

2. **Selecting and Completing Courses:**

- *Identify Skill Gaps:* Take courses that address any gaps or enhance your existing skills relevant to your career goals.

- *Create a Learning Schedule:* Set aside dedicated time each week to complete courses. This helps maintain a steady pace and keeps you motivated.

3. **Certifications and Projects:**

- *Showcase Certifications:* Add completed courses and certifications to your resume, LinkedIn profile, and portfolio to demonstrate your commitment to continuous learning.

- *Capstone Projects:* Use capstone projects or course-related work to build your portfolio and show practical application of your skills.

Real-World Examples and Case Studies

Examining real-world examples of introverts who have successfully used online resources and networks can provide inspiration and practical insights.

Case Study 1: The Freelance Graphic Designer

Jane, an introvert skilled in graphic design, utilized platforms like Upwork and Behance to build her client base and showcase her work. She created a comprehensive portfolio highlighting her best projects, which attracted clients looking for high-quality design work. Jane also joined industry-specific LinkedIn groups to network and stay updated on industry trends. This approach allowed her to work in a quiet, remote setting while steadily growing her freelance business.

Case Study 2: The Software Developer Utilizing LinkedIn

Tom, a software developer who prefers deep focus and minimal social interaction, optimized his LinkedIn profile to reflect his technical skills and accomplishments. He used LinkedIn's job search features to find remote opportunities that matched his expertise.

Tom also participated in LinkedIn discussions related to software development, which led to several job offers and projects. His visibility within the professional network helped him secure a remote role with a tech company that valued independent, focused work.

Conclusion

Utilizing online resources and networks effectively is a powerful strategy for introverts seeking the perfect job. By leveraging job search websites, professional networking sites, virtual job fairs, and online learning platforms, introverts can navigate the job market with confidence and efficiency. Building a strong online presence through portfolios, profiles, and engagement in industry communities further enhances visibility and opportunities. These digital tools enable introverts to connect with potential employers, showcase their skills, and find roles that align with their strengths and preferences, leading to fulfilling and rewarding careers.

Chapter 4

Crafting a Resume Highlighting Introvert Strengths

and The Importance of Tailoring Your Cover Letter

C RAFTING A RESUME THAT truly resonates with hiring managers requires careful consideration, especially for introverts who might have unique strengths that are not easily conveyed through traditional forms. Highlighting introvert-specific strengths effectively involves focusing on qualities like deep focus, analytical thinking, creativity, and the ability to work independently. This section will guide you through crafting a resume that showcases these attributes, ensuring that your true potential shines through.

Understanding Introvert Strengths for Resumes

Introverts possess a number of inherent strengths that can be highly valuable to employers and need to be effectively communicated in a resume. These strengths commonly include:

1. **Deep Focus and Concentration:** Ability to engage in tasks requiring sustained attention.

2. **Analytical Skills:** Keen ability to analyze data and draw insightful conclusions.

3. **Creativity:** Often adept at thinking outside the box and generating innovative ideas.

4. **Independent Work Capability:** Highly capable of working independently without the need for constant supervision.

5. Effective Written Communication: Superior skills in writing clear and detailed reports or correspondence.

6. Detail-Oriented: Attention to the finer details ensuring accuracy and quality.

Structuring Your Resume Effectively

A well-structured resume for an introvert should clearly highlight these strengths while minimizing areas of discomfort, such as excessive personal details. Here's how to structure your resume:

1. Contact Information: List your name, phone number, email address, and LinkedIn profile or personal website if applicable.

2. Professional Summary:

- *Crafting the Summary:* Write a concise, four-to-five-sentence summary that emphasizes your key strengths and achievements.

- *Example:* "Detail-oriented Data Analyst with over 5 years of experience in leveraging analytical tools to drive insights and improve business performance. Skilled in independent work environments and known for delivering high-quality reports with exceptional accuracy."

3. Skills Section:

- *Key Skills:* Highlight skills that align with introverted strengths. Use bullet points for clarity.

- *Example:*

    ○ Attention to Detail

    ○ Analytical Thinking

    ○ Creative Problem Solving

    ○ Independent Work Capability

    ○ Strong Written Communication

○ Deep Focus and Concentration

4. Professional Experience:

- *Format:* List your employment history in reverse chronological order.

- *Detail:* Include job title, company name, location, and dates of employment.

- *Responsibilities and Achievements:* Use bullet points to detail responsibilities and achievements, focusing on those that highlight your introverted strengths.

- *Example:*

- *Data Analyst, XYZ Corporation, New York, NY*

  ○ Conducted in-depth data analysis to support strategic decision-making.

  ○ Produced detailed reports utilizing SQL, Excel, and Tableau.

  ○ Identified trends and delivered actionable insights, leading to a 15% increase in operational efficiency.

5. Education:

- Include degrees, institutions, and graduation dates.

- Highlight relevant coursework or projects that reflect your analytical and creative capabilities.

6. Certifications and Training:

- List any certifications or professional training that emphasize specialized skills.

- Example: "Certified Data Scientist (CDS), completed advanced training in Python and Machine Learning."

Tailoring Your Resume for Specific Jobs

To increase your chances of landing the perfect job, you should tailor your resume for each application, aligning your skills and experiences with the job description.

1. Analysis of Job Description:

- Identify key requirements and preferred qualifications in the job description.

- Example: If a job emphasizes "Strong analytical abilities," make sure this skill is highlighted prominently in your resume.

2. Matching Skills and Keywords:

- Use keywords from the job description throughout your resume to align with the Applicant Tracking System (ATS) software that many companies use.

- Adjust key points in your professional experience to match these keywords.

3. Highlight Relevant Experiences:

- Emphasize projects and tasks that directly relate to the job. If applying for a creative role, focus on projects where you demonstrated innovative thinking.

- *Example:* "Led a project team to develop a creative marketing strategy resulting in a 20% increase in social media engagement."

Showcasing Achievements and Metrics

Employers are interested in measurable achievements. Providing concrete examples and metrics can make your resume stand out.

1. Quantifying Success:

- Whenever possible, quantify your achievements with numbers, percentages, or other concrete metrics.

- *Example:* "Reduced data processing time by 30% through the implementation of automated scripts."

2. Action-Oriented Language:

- Use powerful, action-oriented language to describe your achievements.

- *Example:* "Developed a comprehensive database that streamlined reporting processes, reducing errors by 25%."

3. Listing Notable Accomplishments:

- Create a separate section or integrate these into your work experience.

- *Example:* "Received the 'Employee of the Month' award for exceptional analytical work in Q3 2022."

Leveraging Professional References and Recommendations

Strong professional references and recommendations can add credibility to your resume, offering external validation of your strengths.

1. Choosing References:

- Select references who can speak to your specific strengths and professional abilities.

- *Example:* Former managers, team leaders, or professional mentors.

2. Requesting Recommendations:

- Politely request LinkedIn recommendations or written references.

- Provide your referees with specific examples of your work they can mention.

3. Including References on Your Resume:

- Optionally, include a section at the end of your resume titled "Professional References Available Upon Request" or attach a separate reference sheet if requested.

Design and Formatting Tips

A well-designed resume can make a strong visual impact and ensure readability.

1. Clarity and Readability:

- Use a clean, professional font (e.g., Arial, Times New Roman) and a font size of 10-12 points.

- Ensure adequate white space and use bullet points for easy scanning.

2. Consistent Formatting:

- Maintain consistent formatting throughout the resume. Align dates and job titles, and use the same style for headings and bullet points.

3. Professional Layout:

- Consider using resume templates that offer professional layouts while allowing customization to reflect your personal brand.

4. Proofreading:

- Review your resume multiple times for spelling, grammar, and formatting errors.

- Consider seeking feedback from a trusted friend or using professional resume services for a thorough review.

Example Resumes

To provide a clear visual guide, here are examples of tailored resumes for different roles suited for introverts.

Example 1: Data Analyst Resume

[Your Name]

[Your Address] | [Your Email] | [Your Phone Number] | [LinkedIn Profile]

Professional Summary

Detail-oriented Data Analyst with over 5 years of experience in leveraging analytical tools to drive insights and improve business performance. Skilled in independent work environments and known for delivering high-quality reports with exceptional accuracy.

Key Skills

- Attention to Detail

- Analytical Thinking

- Creative Problem Solving

- Independent Work Capability

- Strong Written Communication

- Deep Focus and Concentration

Professional Experience

Data Analyst | XYZ Corporation, New York, NY | June 2018 – Present

- Conducted in-depth data analysis to support strategic decision-making.

- Produced detailed reports utilizing SQL, Excel, and Tableau.

- Identified trends and delivered actionable insights, leading to a 15% increase in operational efficiency.

Junior Data Analyst | ABC Inc., Boston, MA | January 2015 – May 2018

- Assisted in the development and maintenance of data reporting systems.

- Verified data accuracy and collaborated on quarterly performance reviews.

Education

Bachelor of Science in Data Science | University of Somewhere | Graduated May 2014

Certifications and Training

- Certified Data Scientist (CDS), 2021

- Completed advanced training in Python and Machine Learning

Professional References Available Upon Request

Example 2: Freelance Graphic Designer Resume

[Your Name]

[Your Address] | [Your Email] | [Your Phone Number] | [Portfolio Website]

Professional Summary

Creative and detail-oriented Freelance Graphic Designer with over 7 years of experience producing visually compelling designs. Specialist in independent project management and delivering high-quality work that meets client needs.

Key Skills

- Photoshop and Illustrator Expertise

- Creative Concept Development

- Independent Project Management

- Strong Written Communication

- Deep Focus and Concentration

- Client Collaboration

Professional Experience

Freelance Graphic Designer | Self-Employed | Remote | January 2015 – Present

- Developed branding materials for over 50 clients, resulting in consistent client satisfaction and repeat business.

- Created comprehensive design solutions, including logos, brochures, and digital media campaigns.

- Managed multiple projects simultaneously, meeting all deadlines and exceeding client expectations.

Graphic Design Intern | Creative Agency, Los Angeles, CA | June 2013 – December 2014

- Assisted senior designers in creating marketing materials and campaign visuals.

- Gained hands-on experience in client meetings and project development.

Education

Bachelor of Fine Arts in Graphic Design | Art School of Somewhere | Graduated May 2013

Certifications and Training

- Certified Adobe Illustrator Expert, 2020

- Completed UX Design Certification, 2019

Professional References Available Upon Request

By crafting resumes that emphasize the unique strengths of introverts, you can effectively communicate your value to potential employers. Tailoring your resume for specific jobs, showcasing achievements with concrete metrics, and presenting a well-structured, error-free document will enhance your chances of securing the perfect role. Keep these guidelines in mind as you navigate the job application process, and remember that your introverted qualities are indeed formidable strengths in the workplace.

Tailoring Cover Letters to Specific Jobs

A cover letter is an essential part of any job application, offering a unique opportunity to personalize your application and demonstrate how your qualifications align with the specific needs of the job. For introverts, tailoring a cover letter effectively involves highlighting individual strengths, providing concrete examples, and articulating how your abilities align with the role. This section delves into the best strategies and techniques for crafting a compelling cover letter for specific jobs.

The Importance of Tailoring Your Cover Letter

Tailoring your cover letter to the specific job you're applying for is crucial for several reasons:

1. **Demonstrates Genuine Interest:** A customized cover letter shows that you've taken the time to understand the job and the company, highlighting your genuine interest in the position.

2. **Highlights Key Qualifications:** Personalizing your cover letter allows you to explicitly match your skills and experiences with the job requirements, making it easier for hiring managers to see your fit for the role.

3. **Differentiates You from Other Candidates:** A well-crafted, specific cover letter sets you apart from candidates who submit generic applications.

Analyzing the Job Description

The first step in tailoring your cover letter is to thoroughly analyze the job description. Look for keywords, required skills, and responsibilities to understand what the employer is seeking.

1. **Identify Key Responsibilities and Skills:** Highlight or note down the primary duties and qualifications mentioned in the job description.

   - *Example:* Key responsibilities for a Data Analyst position might include data mining, statistical analysis, and reporting.

2. **Understand Company Values and Culture:** Research the company's website, mission statement, and any recent news or projects to gain insights into their values and work culture.

Structuring Your Cover Letter

A well-structured cover letter includes the following key components:

1. **Header:**

- Include your contact information, the date, and the employer's contact information.

2. **Salutation:**

- Address the hiring manager by name, if possible. If the name isn't provided, use a general greeting like "Dear Hiring Manager."

3. **Introduction:**

- Start with a strong opening sentence that grabs attention. Mention the job you're applying for and where you found the listing.

- *Example:* "I am excited to apply for the Data Analyst position at XYZ Corporation, as advertised on your company website."

4. **Body:**

- *First Paragraph:* Briefly introduce yourself and mention why you're interested in the role. Highlight a relevant achievement or experience.

- *Example:* "With over five years of experience in data analysis, I have developed a keen aptitude for extracting actionable insights from complex datasets, which aligns perfectly with the responsibilities outlined for this role."

- *Second Paragraph:* Provide concrete examples of your skills and achievements that match the job's key requirements.

- *Example:* "At ABC Inc., I led a project that utilized advanced statistical models to optimize our marketing strategies, resulting in a 20% increase in ROI."

- *Third Paragraph:* Reflect on your understanding of the company's goals and explain how your skills and experiences can contribute to their objectives.

- *Example:* "I am particularly impressed by XYZ Corporation's commitment to leveraging data-driven strategies to enhance operational efficiency. My background in developing predictive analytics can support XYZ's ongoing efforts to streamline processes and drive growth."

5. **Conclusion:**

- Summarize your interest in the role and express enthusiasm for the opportunity to discuss your application further.

- *Example:* "I am eager to bring my analytical skills and experience to XYZ Corporation and look forward to the possibility of discussing how I can contribute to your team. Thank you for considering my application."

6. **Signature:**

- Use a professional closing like "Sincerely" or "Best regards," followed by your name.

Using Keywords Effectively

Integrating keywords from the job description into your cover letter can enhance your application's visibility, especially if it passes through an Applicant Tracking System (ATS).

1. **Identify Relevant Keywords:** Extract important keywords from the job description, focusing on skills, qualifications, and responsibilities.

- *Example:* Keywords for a Data Analyst role might include "data mining," "statistical analysis," "SQL," and "reporting."

2. **Incorporate Keywords Naturally:** Weave these keywords into your cover letter in a way that feels natural and cohesive. Avoid keyword stuffing.

- *Example:* "In my previous role, I utilized SQL for data mining and performed statistical analysis to generate detailed reports for executive review."

Highlighting Achievements and Skills

Emphasizing your achievements and relevant skills is crucial for making a strong impression.

1. **Provide Specific Examples:** Use concrete examples to demonstrate how your skills have led to successful outcomes.

- *Example:* "Implemented a new data visualization tool that reduced report generation time by 30% and improved accuracy."

2. **Quantify Achievements:** Where possible, quantify your achievements to provide clear evidence of your impact.

- *Example:* "Analyzed customer data to identify trends, leading to a 15% increase in customer retention rates."

Demonstrating Alignment with Company Values

Research the company's mission, values, and culture, and reflect this understanding in your cover letter.

1. **Show Genuine Interest:** Mention specific aspects of the company that resonate with you and align with your values.

- *Example:* "XYZ Corporation's innovative approach to sustainable business practices greatly appeals to me, as I have a strong commitment to environmental sustainability."

2. **Align Your Skills and Experiences:** Link your professional experiences and skills with the company's goals and initiatives.

- *Example:* "My experience in developing eco-friendly data solutions can contribute to XYZ's sustainability goals, particularly in optimizing resource utilization."

Common Pitfalls to Avoid

When tailoring your cover letter, be mindful of common pitfalls that can undermine your application.

1. **Generic Language:** Avoid using generic or overly formal language that lacks personality and fails to convey your enthusiasm.

2. **Excessive Length:** Keep your cover letter concise, ideally no longer than one page. Focus on the most relevant and impactful information.

3. **Repetition of Resume Content:** Rather than repeating resume details, use the cover letter to expand on key points and provide context for your achievements.

4. **Lack of Proofreading:** Ensure your cover letter is free from spelling and grammatical errors. Consider using tools like Grammarly or seeking feedback from a trusted friend.

Example Cover Letters

To provide practical guidance, here are examples of tailored cover letters for different roles suited for introverts.

Example 1: Data Analyst Cover Letter

[Your Name]

[Your Address]

[Your Email]

[Your Phone Number]

[Date]

[Hiring Manager's Name]

XYZ Corporation

[Company Address]

Dear [Hiring Manager's Name],

I am excited to apply for the Data Analyst position at XYZ Corporation, as advertised on your company website. With over five years of experience in data analysis, I have developed a keen aptitude for extracting actionable insights from complex datasets, which aligns perfectly with the responsibilities outlined for this role.

At ABC Inc., I led a project that utilized advanced statistical models to optimize our marketing strategies, resulting in a 20% increase in ROI. My proficiency in SQL, Excel, and data visualization tools allowed me to generate detailed reports that informed strategic decisions. I believe that my analytical skills and ability to work independently would be a valuable asset to XYZ Corporation.

I am particularly impressed by XYZ Corporation's commitment to leveraging data-driven strategies to enhance operational efficiency. My background in developing predictive analytics can support XYZ's ongoing efforts to streamline processes and drive growth. I am eager to bring my analytical skills and experience to XYZ Corporation and look forward to the possibility of discussing how I can contribute to your team.

Thank you for considering my application. I look forward to the opportunity to speak with you further.

Sincerely,

[Your Name]

Example 2: Freelance Graphic Designer Cover Letter

[Your Name]

[Your Address]

[Your Email]

[Your Phone Number]

[Date]

[Client's Name]

[Client's Company]

[Client's Address]

Dear [Client's Name],

I am writing to express my interest in the freelance graphic designer opportunity at [Client's Company]. With over seven years of experience producing visually compelling designs, I am confident in my ability to deliver high-quality work that meets your needs.

As a freelance graphic designer, I have developed branding materials for over 50 clients, resulting in consistent client satisfaction and repeat business. My expertise in Adobe Photoshop and Illustrator, combined with a strong creative concept development process, allows me to create comprehensive design solutions tailored to each client's vision. I thrive in independent project management and maintain a deep focus on delivering high-quality results.

I am particularly drawn to [Client's Company]'s innovative and client-centric approach to design. I believe my skills in creative problem-solving and attention to detail align well with your company's goals. I am enthusiastic about the opportunity to contribute to your projects and help bring your clients' visions to life.

Thank you for considering my application. I would welcome the chance to discuss how my design skills can benefit [Client's Company]. Please feel free to contact me at your convenience.

Best regards,

[Your Name]

Conclusion

Crafting a tailored cover letter is a critical step in the job application process, particularly for introverts who can leverage their unique strengths and qualities. By thoroughly analyzing the job description, incorporating relevant keywords, providing specific examples, and demonstrating alignment with company values, you can create a compelling cover letter that sets you apart from other candidates. Avoid common pitfalls and keep your cover letter concise and impactful. With these strategies, you can effectively showcase your qualifications and genuine interest, increasing your chances of securing the perfect job.

Chapter 5

Preparing for Common Interview Questions

and Using Introversion as a Strength in Interviews

P REPARING FOR AN INTERVIEW is a crucial step in the job-hunting process, especially for introverts who may find such interactions challenging. Effective preparation can help you present your best self and demonstrate your strengths confidently. Let's guide you through common interview questions and strategies to prepare and respond effectively.

Understanding Common Interview Questions

Interviews often follow a predictable pattern with a set of common questions designed to assess your qualifications, personality, and how well you fit into the company culture. Understanding these questions and preparing your responses in advance can help you navigate the interview more comfortably.

Typical Categories of Interview Questions:

1. Introductory Questions

2. Behavioral Questions

3. Technical or Job-Specific Questions

4. Situational Questions

5. Questions About Your Background and Experience

6. Questions About the Company and Role

7. Questions to Assess Cultural Fit

8. Closing Questions

Sample Common Interview Questions and How to Prepare

1. Introductory Questions

These questions help interviewers get to know you and set the stage for the interview.

- **Tell me about yourself.**

  - *Preparation Tip:* Craft a brief, compelling story that summarizes your professional background, key achievements, and what brings you to this interview. Focus on aspects relevant to the job.

  - *Sample Answer:* "I have over seven years of experience in graphic design, specializing in visual branding and digital media. At my previous job, I led design projects that increased client engagement by 30%. I'm excited about the opportunity to bring my creative skills to XYZ Company, where I can contribute to innovative marketing campaigns."

- **Why are you interested in this position?**

  - *Preparation Tip:* Align your skills and career goals with the job's requirements and the company's mission. Show enthusiasm for the role and how it fits into your career plan.

  - *Sample Answer:* "I am drawn to this role because of XYZ Company's dedication to innovation and sustainability, which aligns with my values. Additionally, my background in data analysis and passion for eco-friendly solutions make this position a perfect fit."

2. Behavioral Questions

These questions will assist the interviewer in understanding how you handle different work situations and challenges based on your past experiences.

- **Can you describe a time when you faced a significant challenge at work**

and how you handled it?

- *Preparation Tip:* Use the STAR method *(Situation, Task, Action, Result)* to structure your response, focusing on the actions you took and the outcomes.

- *Sample Answer:* "At my previous job, we faced a tight deadline to deliver a major client presentation. As the lead analyst, I coordinated with my team to divide tasks efficiently, worked extra hours to ensure data accuracy, and successfully presented our findings, resulting in securing a $500,000 contract."

- **Give an example of when you had to work as part of a team. How did you handle it?**

  - *Preparation Tip:* Highlight your ability to collaborate while also showcasing your independent contributions.

  - *Sample Answer:* "While working on a project to redesign the company website, I collaborated with IT, marketing, and content teams. I took the initiative to create wireframes that incorporated feedback from all departments, leading to a cohesive and user-friendly final design."

3. Technical or Job-Specific Questions

These questions will evaluate your technical skills and knowledge relevant to the job.

- **What tools and techniques do you use for data analysis?**

  - *Preparation Tip:* Provide specific examples of tools and methodologies you employ, emphasizing your proficiency and experience.

  - *Sample Answer:* "I frequently use SQL for database management, Excel for data manipulation, and Tableau for data visualization. Additionally, I employ statistical analysis methods and machine learning algorithms to develop insights from large datasets."

- **Describe your experience with [specific software or tool].**

  - *Preparation Tip:* Be honest about your proficiency level and provide examples of how you've used the tool effectively in past projects.

- *Sample Answer:* "I have extensive experience with Adobe Creative Suite, particularly Photoshop and Illustrator, which I've used to create marketing materials that led to a 25% increase in social media engagement."

4. Situational Questions

These questions assess your problem-solving and decision-making abilities in hypothetical scenarios.

- **How would you handle a situation where you have multiple urgent tasks with tight deadlines?**

  - *Preparation Tip:* Demonstrate your organizational skills, prioritization strategies, and ability to remain calm under pressure.

  - *Sample Answer:* "I would start by assessing the urgency and impact of each task. I would prioritize them accordingly, set a realistic schedule, and possibly delegate tasks when appropriate. By maintaining clear communication with stakeholders and focusing on one task at a time, I could ensure timely and high-quality completion."

5. Questions About Your Background and Experience

These questions delve into your career history, seeking to understand your qualifications and professional journey.

- **Can you walk me through your resume?**

  - *Preparation Tip:* Provide a concise overview of your career progression, highlighting key achievements and transitions that are relevant to the position you are applying for.

  - *Sample Answer:* "I started my career as a junior graphic designer after graduating with a BFA in Graphic Design. Over the years, I advanced to lead designer roles, working on high-profile projects that honed my skills in branding and digital marketing. My previous position at ABC Inc. allowed me to develop and execute campaigns that significantly boosted client engagement and brand visibility."

6. Questions About the Company and Role

These questions test your knowledge and interest in the prospective employer and your understanding of the job.

- **What do you know about our company?**

  - *Preparation Tip:* Research the company's history, mission, values, products, and recent news or achievements. Tailor your response to show genuine interest and alignment with their values.

  - *Sample Answer:* "I understand that XYZ Corporation is at the forefront of sustainable technology innovation, and you've recently been recognized for your groundbreaking work in renewable energy solutions. Your commitment to making a positive environmental influence resonates with my own professional values and goals."

- **Why do you want to work here?**

  - *Preparation Tip:* Connect your career goals and values with the company's mission and the role's responsibilities.

  - *Sample Answer:* "I'm particularly impressed by your dedication to sustainability and innovation. Having worked on various projects focused on eco-friendly solutions, I'm excited about the opportunity to add my skills to a company that mirrors my passion for making a positive impact."

7. Questions to Assess Cultural Fit

These questions determine if you would be a good match for the company's work culture and values.

- **How do you handle working in a team environment where you have differing opinions?**

  - *Preparation Tip:* Highlight your ability to listen, communicate effectively, and find common ground.

- *Sample Answer:* "I believe that differing opinions can lead to stronger solutions. I listen actively to understand different perspectives, communicate my views respectfully, and strive to find consensus or a compromise that benefits the team and project."

- **Describe the work environment that allows you to be most effective.**

  - *Preparation Tip:* Honestly describe the conditions in which you thrive while ensuring it aligns with the company's environment.

  - *Sample Answer:* "I'm most effective in a structured environment that allows for independent work with minimal distractions. I value clear communication and set goals, which help me to focus and perform at my best."

8. Closing Questions

These questions wrap up the interview and can gauge your interest and next steps.

- **Do you have any questions for us?**

  - *Preparation Tip:* Always have a couple of well-thought-out questions prepared that demonstrate your interest in the position and company.

- *Sample Questions:*

  - "Can you tell me more about the team I would be working with?"

  - "What are the next steps in the hiring process?"

  - "How does the company support professional development and career growth?"

Practice Makes Perfect

Consistent practice can significantly improve your confidence and performance in interviews. Here are steps to practice effectively:

1. **Mock Interviews:** Participate in mock interviews with friends, family, or career coaches to simulate the interview environment.

2. **Recording Responses:** Record your responses to common interview questions and review them. This helps you refine your answers and become more comfortable speaking about your experiences.

3. **Reflect and Adapt:** After each practice session, reflect on what went well and what could be improved. Adapt your responses to address any weaknesses.

Leveraging Introversion as a Strength

Introverts possess unique strengths that can be effectively leveraged during interviews:

1. **Deep Thought and Preparation:** Your ability to think deeply and prepare thoroughly can lead to well-considered and insightful responses.

2. **Listening Skills:** Use your strong listening skills to understand the questions fully and respond thoughtfully.

3. **Written Follow-Up:** If you feel you could have communicated certain points better, a well-crafted thank-you email can clarify these points and reinforce your interest in the role.

Using Introversion as a Strength in Interviews

Introversion is often seen as a disadvantage in interviews, which typically favor outgoing and talkative individuals. However, introverts can turn their natural tendencies into strengths and excel in job interviews by leveraging their unique attributes. This section provides strategies for using introversion as an asset during the interview process.

Emphasizing Strengths Inherent to Introverts

Introverts possess several qualities that can be highlighted as strengths during an interview.

1. **Preparation and Attention to Detail:** Introverts typically excel in preparation and pay close attention to detail. Demonstrate your thorough preparation by being well-versed with the company's background, job description, and industry trends.

- *Example:* "I've researched XYZ Corporation's recent projects extensively and understand that you're currently focusing on expanding into renewable energy markets. My prior experience with eco-friendly data solutions and sustainability consulting would align well with these initiatives."

2. **Deep Listening and Thoughtful Responses:** Introverts are excellent listeners and tend to offer thoughtful, well-considered responses. Use this to your advantage by actively listening to interviewers and providing concise, insightful answers.

- *Example:* "Based on your focus on operational efficiency, I would approach this challenge by conducting a thorough analysis of existing processes and identifying areas for optimization. In my previous role, this approach led to a 15% increase in productivity."

3. **Independent Work and Self-Motivation:** Highlight your ability to work independently and stay motivated without constant supervision. Emphasize experiences where you successfully managed projects or tasks on your own.

- *Example:* "In my last position, I spearheaded a project to develop a new data management system. Working independently, I was able to complete the project ahead of schedule, which resulted in improved data accuracy and accessibility for the team."

Strategies for Introverts During Interviews

Adopting specific strategies can help introverts present themselves confidently and effectively during interviews.

1. **Structured Responses:** Use structured response techniques like the STAR method *(Situation, Task, Action, Result)* to provide clear and organized answers.

- *Example:* "In my previous role (Situation), I was tasked with leading a team project under tight deadlines (Task). I devised a structured plan, assigned specific roles to team members, and monitored progress regularly (Action). As a result, we completed the project two days ahead of schedule, earning positive feedback from the client (Result)."

2. **Pause and Reflect:** Take a moment to pause and reflect before answering questions. This shows you're considering your response carefully and avoids the pressure of immediate answers.

- *Example:* "That's a great question. Let me take a moment to think about the best example to share."

3. **Personal Stories and Examples:** Share personal stories or examples that highlight your strengths and approach to work. These can make your responses more memorable and relatable.

- *Example:* "One memorable project involved developing a comprehensive report on market trends. I spent several weeks compiling data, analyzing trends, and creating detailed visualizations. This report was well-received and used to guide our strategic planning for the next quarter."

4. **Leverage Strengths in Written Communication:** As an introvert, you might excel in written communication. Follow up your interview with a well-crafted thank-you email that reiterates your interest and highlights key points from the interview.

- *Example:* "Thank you for taking the time to discuss the Data Analyst position with me today. I am excited about the opportunity to contribute to XYZ Corporation's innovative projects and believe my analytical skills and commitment to sustainability would be a great fit. Please feel free to reach out if you require any further information."

Managing Interview Anxiety

Interview anxiety is common, particularly for introverts. Developing strategies to manage this anxiety can help you perform better.

1. **Practicing Mindfulness and Breathing Techniques:** Techniques like deep breathing, mindfulness, and guided meditation can help calm nerves and maintain focus.

- *Example:* Practice deep breathing exercises before the interview to reduce anxiety and center yourself.

2. **Arriving Prepared and Punctual:** Arriving well-prepared and punctual can reduce anxiety and create a sense of control.

- *Example:* "Arrive at the interview location 15 minutes early to familiarize yourself with the environment and gather your thoughts."

3. **Positive Visualization:** Visualize a successful interview experience. Imagine yourself answering questions confidently, engaging positively with interviewers, and leaving a strong impression.

- *Example:* Spend a few minutes visualizing the interview scenario, from introductions to answering questions confidently.

4. **Seeking Support and Feedback:** Discuss your anxieties with a trusted friend or mentor who can offer support and constructive feedback.

- *Example:* "Arrange a mock interview with a mentor who can provide feedback and help you build confidence."

Highlighting Introversion as a Strength Directly

When appropriate, directly addressing your introverted nature and framing it as a strength can be impactful.

1. **Honesty and Authenticity:** Be honest about your introverted tendencies and explain how they contribute positively to your work.

- *Example:* "As an introvert, I find that I excel in roles that require deep focus and analytical thinking. I have a unique ability to concentrate on complex problems and produce high-quality, detailed work."

2. **Connecting to Job Requirements:** Link your introverted strengths directly to the job requirements to show alignment.

- *Example:* "This role requires meticulous attention to detail and independent work, both of which are my strong suits. I am confident in my ability to manage large datasets and produce insightful analysis consistently."

3. **Positive Framing:** Frame your introverted traits in a positive light, emphasizing their benefits.

- *Example:* "One of my key strengths is my ability to listen and understand different perspectives. This has helped me to build strong working relationships and contribute effectively in team settings."

Real-World Examples and Case Studies

Examining real-world examples of introverts who have leveraged their strengths in interviews can provide practical insights and inspiration.

Case Study 1: The Analytical Thinker

Sarah, an introverted data analyst, prepared for her job interview by thoroughly researching the company and practicing structured responses. During the interview, she highlighted her analytical skills, attention to detail, and ability to work independently. When asked about her approach to team projects, Sarah shared a specific example of how she successfully led a data analysis project, emphasizing her leadership and organizational skills. Her thoughtful responses and clear alignment with the job requirements impressed the interviewers, leading to a job offer.

Case Study 2: The Creative Problem-Solver

John, a creative introvert applying for a graphic designer position, used his portfolio to showcase his best work and prepared to discuss the creative process behind each project. During the interview, he highlighted his ability to generate innovative ideas and work autonomously. John shared stories of how he developed branding materials that exceeded client expectations and increased engagement. His detailed descriptions of his work process and tangible results demonstrated his value, securing him the job.

Conclusion

Using introversion as a strength in interviews requires understanding and leveraging the unique qualities you bring to the table. By emphasizing inherent strengths, employing effective strategies, and managing anxiety, introverts can navigate the interview process with confidence and showcase their true potential. Honest and authentic communication about your introverted nature, coupled with concrete examples of how it benefits your work, can leave a lasting positive impression on interviewers. With thorough preparation and a focus on your strengths, you can effectively use introversion as an asset to succeed in job interviews and secure the perfect job.

Chapter 6

Final Thoughts

and Encouragement for the Journey Ahead

A S WE REACH THE conclusion of "*The Introvert's Tips to Find the Perfect Job*," it's crucial to reflect on the journey we've traversed together. This guide has walked you through the various stages of understanding your introverted nature, assessing your strengths and weaknesses, exploring suitable job options, tailoring your job applications, acing interviews, and ultimately embracing your introversion as a powerful asset in your professional life.

Embracing Introversion

One of the most significant takeaways from this guide is recognizing and embracing your introverted nature. Introversion is not a hindrance; rather, it's a unique quality that, when understood and utilized correctly, can lead to a fulfilling and successful career. Understanding your introverted nature allows you to:

1. **Identify and Leverage Strengths:** Your ability to focus deeply, think analytically, and work independently are invaluable strengths in many professional roles. By recognizing these attributes, you can seek out and thrive in positions that value meticulousness, creativity, and critical thinking.

2. **Navigate Social Interactions with Confidence:** While introverts may find large social gatherings draining, smaller, more meaningful interactions can be highly rewarding. Leveraging platforms that align with your communication preferences, like one-on-one meetings or written correspondence, can maximize your networking effectiveness.

3. **Optimize Your Work Environment:** Whether working remotely, in a quiet office space, or collaborating within small teams, understanding your preferred work environment can significantly enhance your job satisfaction and productivity.

The Path to Self-Improvement

The journey towards finding the perfect job is also one of personal growth and self-improvement. Here are some continuous self-improvement strategies that can help maintain and enhance your professional journey:

1. **Continuous Learning:** The job market is ever-evolving, and staying updated with new skills and trends is crucial. Engage in lifelong learning through online courses, workshops, and professional development programs to keep your skill set relevant and competitive.

2. **Networking:** Although networking can be challenging, building a strong network of professional contacts can open doors to new opportunities. Focus on quality over quantity—seek meaningful connections rather than broad networks.

3. **Self-Care:** Remember that professional success does not have to come at the expense of personal well-being. Prioritize self-care, ensure a healthy work-life balance, and find time for activities that rejuvenate you.

Realizing Your Potential

The ultimate goal of this guide is to help you find a job that not only suits your skills but also resonates with your values and passions. Realizing your potential requires:

1. **Setting Clear Goals:** Define what career success looks like for you. Is it about making a difference, achieving financial stability, or working in an area you're passionate about? Setting clear, achievable goals can guide your job search process.

2. **Staying Resilient:** The job search process can be daunting, with rejections along the way. Stay resilient, maintain a positive outlook, and view challenges as opportunities for growth.

3. **Being Proactive:** Take charge of your career path. Don't wait for opportunities to come to you; actively seek them out. Whether through networking, continuous education, or applying to roles that excite you, proactive career management is essential.

Reflecting on Success Stories

Throughout this guide, we've incorporated numerous case studies and real-life examples of introverts who have navigated the job market successfully. Reflecting on these stories can offer inspiration and practical insights:

1. **Learning from Others:** Observing how others overcame challenges can provide practical strategies that you can adapt to your own context.

2. **Drawing Inspiration:** Stories of success can be motivating. They remind you that finding a fulfilling job is possible and that your introverted nature can be a significant asset.

3. **Building a Community:** Engaging with communities of like-minded professionals, both online and offline, can provide support, camaraderie, and shared learning experiences.

Next Steps

Now that you've absorbed expert tips and strategies to find the perfect job, the next steps involve taking action:

1. **Implement What You've Learned:** Start by updating your resume and LinkedIn profile to highlight your strengths. Tailor your cover letters for each job application, practice common interview questions, and attend networking events that align with your preferences.

2. **Seek Support:** Don't hesitate to seek support from career counselors, mentors, or professional networks. They can provide valuable insights, advice, and connections.

3. **Stay Updated and Adapt:** The job market is dynamic. Stay updated on industry trends, continuously adapt your strategies, and remain open to new opportunities.

Conclusion

In conclusion, *"The Introvert's Tips to Find the Perfect Job"* offers a comprehensive roadmap for introverts navigating the job market. By embracing your unique qualities, leveraging your strengths, and continuously improving, you can not only find but also thrive in a job that truly resonates with your personal and professional aspirations. The journey might be challenging, but with the right approach and mindset, it is entirely within your reach to achieve career fulfillment.

Let this guide be a companion and a source of encouragement as you embark on the path to finding the perfect job, celebrating your introverted nature, and realizing your full potential.

Encouragement for the Journey Ahead

As we come to the end of *"The Introvert's Tips to Find the Perfect Job,"* it's essential to offer encouragement for the journey ahead. The process of finding the right job can be daunting, and it's natural to face uncertainties and setbacks along the way. However, armed with the right strategies, self-awareness, and resilience, introverts can navigate this journey successfully and emerge stronger and more fulfilled. This concluding section aims to inspire and motivate you as you embark on or continue your pursuit of the perfect job.

Celebrating Your Unique Qualities

Your introverted nature comes with unique strengths that are highly valuable in the professional world. It's crucial to recognize and celebrate these qualities:

1. **Depth of Thought:** Your ability to think deeply and reflect thoroughly is a significant asset. This quality allows you to approach problems with a comprehensive understanding and offer well-considered solutions.

2. **Focus and Attention to Detail:** You excel in environments that require concentration and meticulous attention to detail. These skills are indispensable in fields that demand precision, such as research, data analysis, and creative arts.

3. **Empathy and Listening Skills:** Your natural inclination towards listening and understanding others fosters strong, meaningful relationships. This trait is particularly valued in roles that require interpersonal sensitivity, such as counseling, human resources, and client relations.

Building Confidence and Resilience

Confidence and resilience are key to overcoming challenges in the job search process. Here are some strategies to build and maintain these vital attributes:

1. **Positive Self-Affirmation:** Regularly affirm your strengths and past achievements. Remind yourself of the value you bring to potential employers.

- *Tip:* Keep a journal of your successes and positive feedback received from colleagues, mentors, or clients. Reflect on it whenever you need a confidence boost.

2. **Embracing Failure as a Learning Opportunity:** View setbacks not as failures but as opportunities for growth. Each rejection or difficult interview is a chance to learn and improve.

- *Tip:* After an interview, take note of what went well and areas for improvement. Use this as a guide for future interviews.

3. **Seeking Support:** Don't hesitate to lean on your support network, whether family, friends, mentors, or professional groups. Having a support system can provide the encouragement and advice you need to stay motivated.

- *Tip:* Join online forums or local meet-ups for introverts in your field. Sharing experiences and tips can be incredibly reassuring and empowering.

Taking Proactive Steps

Taking proactive steps in your job search can significantly impact your success. Here are some practical actions to consider:

1. **Networking on Your Terms:** Engage in networking activities that align with your comfort zone. This might include online networking via LinkedIn, participating in industry-specific forums, or attending smaller, more focused networking events.

- *Tip:* Set a goal to connect with a certain number of professionals each month. Start with informational interviews or join online webinars where you can contribute to discussions.

2. **Continuously Updating Your Skills:** Stay ahead in your field by continuously updating your skills through courses, certifications, and workshops.

- *Tip:* Allocate time each week for learning, whether it's watching industry webinars, taking online courses on platforms like Coursera or Udemy, or reading relevant books and articles.

3. **Customizing Applications:** Tailor each resume and cover letter to the specific job to highlight your most relevant skills and experiences.

- *Tip:* Create a master resume that includes all your experiences and skills. Customize this template for each job application by highlighting the sections most relevant to the job description.

Maintaining Work-Life Balance

Finding the right job isn't just about professional fulfillment; it's also about maintaining a healthy work-life balance. This balance is crucial for sustaining long-term success and well-being.

1. **Setting Boundaries:** Ensure you set clear boundaries between work and personal time. This is particularly important if you are working remotely or in a flexible environment.

- *Tip:* Create a dedicated workspace at home and establish a routine that includes regular breaks and a defined end to the workday.

2. **Prioritizing Self-Care:** Make self-care a priority to manage stress and prevent burnout. This includes physical activities, hobbies, meditation, and spending time with loved ones.

- *Tip:* Schedule regular self-care activities into your calendar, just like you would a work meeting, to ensure you make time for them.

3. **Pursuing Hobbies and Interests:** Engaging in activities you enjoy can provide a valuable mental break and rejuvenate you for tackling professional challenges.

- *Tip:* Try new hobbies or revisit old ones that you're passionate about. Whether it's painting, playing a musical instrument, or hiking, make time for these activities regularly.

Looking to the Future

Finally, maintain a forward-looking perspective. Career building is an ongoing journey, and each experience, whether positive or challenging, contributes to your growth.

1. **Setting Long-Term Goals:** Define clear long-term career goals and break them down into smaller, manageable steps. This will provide a roadmap and keep you motivated.

- *Tip:* Use tools like vision boards or career planning apps to visualize and track your career objectives and milestones.

2. **Staying Adaptable:** The job market is dynamic, and being adaptable can open up new opportunities. Stay open to potential career shifts and new directions.

- *Tip:* Regularly review and reflect on your career path. Are there new skills you can learn? Is there a different role or industry that interests you? Keep an open mind.

3. **Celebrating Small Wins:** Celebrate your progress, no matter how small. Acknowledging your achievements, whether landing an interview, completing a course, or making a new professional connection, will keep you motivated.

- *Tip:* Keep a "success journal" where you note down all your achievements and milestones. Reflect on it periodically to see how far you've come.

Conclusion

To all the introverts embarking on or continuing their journey to finding the perfect job, remember that your qualities are your strengths. By leveraging your unique attributes, taking proactive steps, and maintaining a balanced and forward-looking approach, you can confidently navigate the job market and achieve professional fulfillment.

The journey may have its ups and downs, but with resilience, self-awareness, and continuous self-improvement, the perfect job is within your reach. Embrace your introverted nature, celebrate your successes, and keep looking ahead with optimism and determination.

Your journey is just beginning, and the best is yet to come. Keep moving forward with courage and conviction, and you'll find a job that genuinely resonates with your skills, values, and passions. Best of luck on your journey to finding the perfect job. Remember: Your introversion is a powerful asset that can lead you to achieve great things.

Please Rate and Review our Books!

Follow us on social media @aberstoat:

- Instagram

- Tiktok

- Facebook

Books by Q.T. Archer:

- Enrich Your Life: Top Hobbies for Men Over 50

- The Introvert's Tips for Finding the Perfect Job

- Empowering Pursuits for Every Woman *(coming soon)*

www.ingramcontent.com/pod-product-compliance
Lightning Source LLC
Chambersburg PA
CBHW071510210326
41597CB00018B/2715